A Study on Life

Anya Lewinski

A STUDY ON LIFE

A STUDY ON LIFE

"Life is a dream, death the reality."

CONTENTS

The World

The world is a canvas,
a beautiful painting,
the sun, the stars,
moon and sky,
flowers and grass,
water and light,
beautiful in the day
and seen anew at night.

Morning Dew

The sun rises over the hill,
the fields glitter like diamonds,
the stars have fallen from the sky,
and come to rest on the leaves and grass of the meadow.

Birds sing and flowers dance,
sound and sent carried on the wind,
like a scene from a fairytale,
inscribed on the earth.
Only a second, a glimpse, a glance,
of the world God created
where angels dance.

Silver Stars

Silver stars they fill the night
bathing the world in a warm light.

They light the way, and hear us pray
in hopes for a better day.

They tell a story, that rides the wind
and will forever roam
hearing every sin.

They hold secrets that will never be told
eternity hides within their folds.

They are heavens gates held open wide
so that we may have a peek inside.

They know our fate which may hide from us
but to them it's almost obvious.

Our secrets, our desires
our hopes and dreams,
these are the things we hope to be.

So when you look up, at the night sky
and watch the stars as they're passing by,
remember, that all you are
is written upon a silver star.

Wander

Root yourself to the earth
and reach for the heavens,

dig deep in your soul
and find what matters,

feel the stars move above you
and the ground shift below,

watch the moon through its phases
and the tides that she rises.

Be the seeker
the finder
dreamy eyed
with wonder,

be the nomad
who is free
or the wizened
who believes,

wander the world
with an open mind
light heart
joyful spirit,

because those who are lost
do not always wander
and those who wander
are not always lost.

Morning Sunshine

It's quiet,
the air is still
and cool
the birds begin to sing
the worlds alarm clock,
waking the sun from its slumber
as it slowly rises into the sky
from its peaceful resting place
among the stars.

The green of the earth
stretch their leaves to the sky
soaking up the morning sunshine,

then the rich smell of morning coffee
the soft clang of dishes,
padding of slippers,
rustle of sheets,
as the people of the world
wake from their sleep.

You sit in a small corner cafe
nestled at the end of the street,
you see the bookstore across the way
flip on its lights,
one car
then two
then three
as the streets begin to bustle,
another cup is set in front of you
by the kind waitress who's been there all night
and together you watch the world wake.

Cityscape

It's very loud,
always loud,
the constant rumble of traffic
It never sleeps
never dulls
like an eternal migraine.

And there's a pulse to it
like the beating of a heart
as it moves the lifeblood
of a city through its veins.

But there are moments
when everything slows
and everything quiets
down to a whisper
and the sun makes the buildings
glitter like diamonds
and the moon
makes them shine like stars.

The organism truly comes to life
in those few moments,
it shows itself in all its glory
through the colors of the cars in the streets
and the people as they walk,
the buzz in the air
and the undertone of everyone
breathing in unison.

And that's how a city breaths
how a city lives
how a city is.

Ancient Mysteries

Looming stone walls
hewn from the rock
with perfect symmetry,

years of history
written on the surface of the earth,
carved into her skin
tattooed onto her face,

the structure is grand
majestic
magnificent,
an ancient wonder
a modern miracle to behold.

Whispers from the past
of things done right
civilization at its peak,

and as the wheel of time turns
our cities will crumble
civilization will fall,
then once again
will we turn to the earth
and paint our story
onto her walls.

Desert Sands

When desert sands
ride the wind
golden beads of dust and land,

close your eyes
and let it pass
like the sands of time
in an hourglass,

the wind has a way
of revealing to you
things that were lost
beneath the dunes,

ancient mysteries
fortune and ruins
look to the sky
a storm is brewing,

and then it's gone
in the blink of an eye
the desert sands
blowing by.

The Whispering Wood

Stand still,
still as a tree
as a mid-summer breeze
blows gently through the leaves.

Be calm,
calm as the brook
water flowing lazily
as the deer are grazing.

Be quiet,
quiet as a mouse
as it scurries through the brush
always in a rush.

And listen,
listen to the sound
of the forest around,
it speaks in subtle ways
lush and green
sights unseen
by human eyes
in centuries.

Listen,
the wood has a story
to whisper in your ear
so be tranquil
there is nothing to fear.

Ancient branches creak and groan
telling you you're not alone,
the ancient trees tell a tale
ancient stories never fail,
and as they speak
spirits roam
welcoming you
into their home,
and once the tale of trees is through
the forest
will deliver you.

Truths

The thing we all want to be told
but no one wants to hear

Villain

Villain.
What is a villain?
A character whose evil actions or motivations are important to the plot;
someone who is vilified;
an evil person.
But what makes a villain?
Are they born or are they made?
You have to wonder what happened along the way,
to make them a villain in your eyes.
You have to wonder what happened along the way,
to make them a villain in the world's eyes.
And you have to wonder:
is there someone out there who sees them as something more,
who sees them as something else?
Do they know what happened along the way?
Have they seen what happened before?
They know that a villain is not born,
they know a villain is made.
They see, they understand, and it makes them sad,
that the world sees a villain.
A villain is someone whose story has yet to be told.
A villain was first a victim.
We are all a villain in someone's story,
so in the end, it doesn't matter what you've done,
what matters is who's telling the story.

Reasons

Death gives a reason to live.

Humanity

In today's world
it's easy to see,
God's biggest mistake
was humanity.
Thinking this way,
looking down that road,
is a dangerous,
and terrifying thing to behold.
But it's hard to believe,
That an artist such as he,
could make a mistake
such as humanity.
So I think it's safe to say,
clear to see,
that maybe God's greatest triumph,
Was creating you and me.

Fate

The wisps will guide your way
and help you find your fate, they say.

But fate's not something you can search for,
it's something you must find
something hidden deep within,
something that's inside.

In each and every person,
in our hearts and minds,
something that will guide our souls
and reveal itself in time.

It's written in the stars
and rides the fleeting wind,
it surrounds us on every side
and tells us how and when.

It won't define who you are
or who you will become,
it changes like the rising tides
till the earth and you are one.

It leads us on,
till break of dawn,
and will choose our dying day

that's the day when you will find
something that's inside,
in each and every person,
in our hearts and minds,
something that will guide our souls
till the end of time.

Spirited Away

A gentle whisper
a quiet sin
it calls aloud
riding the wind.

It blows the leaves
and travels the breeze
it glides the earth
and skims the seas.

Falling stars that fill the sky
tell a tale that never lies.

The sound of souls
that are whisked away
will vanish forever at break of day.

Then infinity sing's
and Heaven's cry
for a long-lost song that will never die.

A Dark Place

The sun, the moon,
the sky, the stars,
the land and the sea.
The warm spring air
and cool fall breeze.

The family you love
and the friends you adore,
be thankful for these things
they are the light you have in this world.

Be thankful you have them
because others do not.

The dark of night,
the cold of winter,
the shadows, the pain, the loss and sorrow.

They know no love
and wander the world aimlessly,
to find what they have lost
and may never have again.
These are those dark places
where the sun never shines
and the land is barren.

These are the sad places
that most never come back from.
So be grateful for that light you have
even only a sliver
because there is always someone out there
in a darker place than you.

Imagination

Imagine if there were a place,
a place where all your dreams become realities,
every wish granted,
every thought and word that was ever uttered
would take on a shape and form.
It would dance in the wind
and bring music to your ears.

This is a place that is hidden yet not,
can't be found unless you stop looking,
the seekers will not find
but the finders will have been sought.
This is the rule for all places of its kind.

No one can find it except those who already have.
You must be lost to know where you are going
yet those who know where they are going are not lost.
These are the tricks that are played in our minds.
They drive some mad but enlighten others.
You have to be blind to see it
and deaf to hear it.
The smart don't understand it
so the dumb can comprehend it.
Those who can see are blind to it
and those who can hear are deaf to it.

They say a long time ago every soul that walked this earth could find it.
All could see it
all could hear it.
But as the years went on
our senses became numb to it.
We could no longer find,
nor hear,
nor see.
It was instead replaced by the horrors of our world.
Peace with war.
Happiness with depression.
Kindness with cruelty.
Selfless with selfishness.
Moral and immoral.
There was then no right or wrong
or we just couldn't decide which was which.

So we argued and fought.
And that's why this perfect world,
our peace,
quiet, serenity, tranquility
were lost into the depths of the forgotten.

But there are those few
who can still see and hear.
Who dance and sing
to the music of that long-lost wind.
Who turn their dreams into reality
and believe in their fantasies.
They are the strongest even if they don't show it.
They are the ones who are silenced.
They are told to face reality.
To stop dreaming.
To wake up.
They are told to fear and to hide.
To never think and never do.
They are confined
and told to sit
and never get back up.
But the truly brave never give up.
The dreamers don't stop dreaming
the believers don't stop believing
the singers sing
the dancers dance
and they follow their heart.

Waves

It comes in waves,
you can go days without feeling it
forgetting it
but it always comes back.

It only appears after
the person is gone
and stays long into the night,
once it's there it never leaves
even when they come back.

You look them in the eye
and you see it,
every last detail.
You feel it
every last point
of the arrows being driven
through your heart.

Guilt, regret, loneliness
because of what you never said
and empty because of what you did.
The love is still there
but the shadow is too.

You can go days without feeling it
years forgetting it,
but it always comes back
it comes in waves.

Relationships

An unavoidable aspect of life,
impossible to ignore
easy to create
hard to maintain
and way to complicated
for humanities short rein.

Friends for Life

When the sun rises
and the moon sets
You will be there.

When the crickets begin to chirp
and the stars begin to shine
You will be there.

On Christmas eve and easter day
on thanksgiving and in May
You will be there.

On the day I leave for college
and the night of my first kiss
You will be there.

In the summer and the winter
the fall and the spring
an my wedding day
in the rain
and everywhere I go
You will be there.

When We Were Young

Fresh, fun, free
these are the things
a friendship should be.

Forever, fleeting, forgot
there are the things
a friendship is not.

Playful, perfect, planned,
these are the things
many friendships had.

Long, loving, lasting
these are the things
most friendships are lacking.

When we were young,
innocent as can be
a friend can be anybody

Middle School BS

There was a day
when boys became boys
and girls became girls,

there was no warning
just a shove,
and suddenly we couldn't just be friends.

That's when life became complicated
when eyes began to open
when the world began to seep in
and children began to grow up.

Annoying, how that happens,
the girls discover makeup
and the boys discover girls
and the girls discover boys
and the boys discover personal hygiene.

Interesting, how the separation happens,
a boy and a girl can't just be friends
because now people feel the need
to get in the way
and make things awkward.

We forget how to be friends,
the natural flow of things
what it was like before,
because biology gets in the way
and we have to relearn
how relationships work.

Best Friends

We weren't born into the same house
but that didn't keep us apart,

partners in crime
sisters in arms
I got your back
and you got mine.

We share a bond we can't explain
I read your thoughts
you finish my sentences
and even when we're apart
we call at the same time.

Letters of Thanks and Complaints

Music blasts from the stereo
something old, your favorite
the wind blows my hair in every direction
warm and free as I try to tame it.
I fight to pull it back and you laugh at my struggle
I can't help but smile,
you really are terrible

I remember the first day I saw you
the first day we met
to be honest,
you scared me half to death.

This tall imposing figure,
whose morality was unmatched
you seemed all high and mighty
and quite frankly, I was annoyed by that.

I used every tactic,
every trick and every try,
to get a rise from you
but you just let it fly.

Then one day everything changed
we had a little chat.
you looked at me and I at you
I realized you weren't all that.

I learned an important lesson
as our friendship began to grow
that though you see what's outside
most people you don't know.

We have an odd friendship,
you and I.
Expectations and rules
things we won't let by.

I guess I didn't see that
until it was too late
I said a few things, made a mistake

I missed a que, a look, a plea
something I didn't realize you needed from me.

We are similar in many ways
probably too many to count
that's why I missed it
but made it easy to figure out.

Now all I ask, rather simply,
is that next time
you be honest with me

I don't expect much
just a simple yes or no
if you're really ok, then fine
I'll go.

But don't expect me to sympathize
or leave you alone
when for a week you told me yes
when the answer was no.

You've asked me to trust you
with things about myself
worries, fears, beliefs, pains
but how can I?
When you put those things on a shelf.

Out of my reach
away from my view
"I'm always here if you need me"
well same to you.

I thank you for those times,
those lengthy conversations,
they made me think, change my life
brought me confirmation.

I wish to do the same
for all of my friends
but these relationships are built on trust
and that something you didn't extend.

The stereo blares,

wind in my hair,
I'll sit here in silence
and wait for you to share.

Thinking of You

1. Two years…

2. It's been two years

3. But I can't stop thinking

4. An endless loop

5. Around and around and around

6. An endless loop

7. I can't stop thinking

8. Distractions are nice

9. A nice distraction

10. But it always comes back

11. An endless loop

12. I can't stop thinking

13. Two options

14. I have two option

15. You have two options

16. We have two options?

17. Two years

18. The amount of time I've been stalling

19. Two years

20. The amount of time you've been away

21. Two years

22. How long I've been thinking

23. Can't stop thinking

24. An endless loop

25. Two answers

26. Two words

27. I want to get better

28. I want to feel better

29. But I can't stop thinking

30. I should say something

31. I need to say something

32. Stuck in an endless loop

33. Around and around and around

34. Two outcomes

35. Two ways to get out of this endless loop

36. Around and around and around

37. STOP

38. It only took me two years

39. I can break the loop without you

Cleansing Rain

Lift your face to the sky,
close your eyes,
feel the rain wash over you.
Cool, calm, refreshing.
Feel it wash away the stains of the earth,
feel it cleanse the soul,
clean the mind,
and replenish the body.
Water gives life,
water takes it away,
and the rain cleanses the pain.

What is Love?

I know what love is,
the kind I give to my family

I know what love is,
the kind I give to my friends

I know what love is,
the kind I show to strangers

I know what love is,
the kind I show myself.

I don't know what love is,
the kind you find in fairytales

I don't know what love is,
the kind the poets write about

I don't know what love is,
the kind that people die for

I don't know what love is,
the kind that people live for.

What is love?
Is it something you fall into?

What is love?
Is it something you find?

What is love?
Is it something you feel?

What is love?
Or is it a choice?

Letter to My Future Loved One

There are things I want to show you,
memories I hold,
things that will help you understand me
and the stories you've been told.

I want you to see where I grew up,
where I found myself,
the place where I met God
who loves like no one else.

See the joy on my face
as we race through the halls,
the laughter that comes
when somebody falls,

the tears that fall
at memories of times past,
and the satisfaction of knowing
I am home at last.

Meet my mentors, my teachers and friends,
follow me through the labyrinth we call a church
where awe and wonder never end.

That is what I wish for you to see,
the foundation I was build on,
the things that made me,
so that maybe, just maybe
when the sun sets that night,
you will finally see me for me,
I will shine in a new light.

A STUDY ON LIFE

Tragedy

An event causing great
suffering, destruction, distress
a story with an unhappy ending
the downfall of a hero.

The crumbling of a city
destruction of a nation
a word dipped in sarcasm
for any occasion.

When a child falls
when a villain is made
when all the world can feel
is pain.

From that point of view,
the greatest tragedy
ever written
is human history.

Stolen

A girl sits and stares,
"Are you alright?" they ask,
"Yes".

Yet she still weeps,
the tears still fall,
the pain never fades.

He catches her one night,
and asks her what's wrong,
"The feeling", she says,
"will never be gone".

When they took her that night,
all was quiet.
She felt alone, trapped, weak, abandoned, helpless, scared, cold, hopeless.

"I never want to feel that way again,
and I never want to be touched".

The boy nods,
tears in their eyes,
the girl lost something that night,
that can never be returned.

Pouring Rain

Drip drop, drip drop,
the rain falls down.

Flash boom, flash boom,
the thunder sounds.

A still body,
a silent mind,
a restless spirit passing by,
the wind howls,
the shudders shake,

Drip drop, drip drop,
the poor soul will never wake.

Flash boom, flash boom,
the blood is washed away in rain.

The Mountains Echoed

And the mountains echoed with their screams,
the laughter rang out across the fields,
children play,
while mothers sway,
all in the morning breeze.
Life is simple, peaceful, calm.

Then they come,
and ruin it all,
men beaten,
women taken,
children stolen,
never waking,
and before the dust settled,
carried on the morning breeze,
the mountains echoed with their screams.

Fears

Things we deem dangerous
harmful, painful, threatening
adrenaline pumping moments
the mind perceives to be real,
moments the mind can't comprehend,
distortion of reality,
an instinct to survive.

Nightmares

Every night I wake in a cold sweat.
Heart racing,
mind buzzing,
heavy breathing,
voice screaming.

Images flash through my mind,
terrifying.
I switch on the light
and look around.

They're gone
but they will come back.
They haunt me every night.
Lurking in the shadows
waiting for me to fall asleep.

Then they invade my mind
and haunt my dreams.
They are the never ending terror of nightmares,
and these nightmares are mine.

Hidden Faces

Sometimes I wonder if people see me,
like really see me.
Do they see the love, joy and laughter,
or the pain, sorrow and despair?
The emotion that passes across my face
and through my life.
Or do they only see the sarcasm,
the quick wit, smart comebacks,
negative remarks and cold demeanor.
Do they see through the cracks
to the broken girl who always fights to get back up
and tries to shield herself from the world.
Take away the cockiness, overconfidence and indifference,
will they see blonde hair, blue eyes and a pretty face,
or will they see me?

Forgotten

Have you ever heard someone say,
"People die every day"?
Did you ever realize
that they just made those people's lives
completely meaningless?
saying that "People die every day"
they have single handedly thrown those lives out the window
without a second glance
and walked away.

I asked myself a question,
"What is your greatest fear?"
the answer wasn't spiders
or the dark
or death.
Those things scare me but,
my greatest fear is being forgotten.

I don't want to leave this world
and have contributed nothing to it.
I don't want to leave knowing
that I did nothing with my life.
That my life was meaningless
and that at my funeral someone will say
"It's ok. People die every day."
I don't want people to forget about me.
So if your fear is as great as mine
go do something that matters
so that when those bells ring on your last day,
someone will say,
"They will never be forgotten."

Shadows in the Dark

A lot of people say
that they fear the dark,

but that's far from the truth
which is something much more stark

the dark is a suggestion
of something much more sinister.

A little tug or pull,
in the back of your mind,
a warning that there's something else
hidden deep inside.

In contrast to the light
where everything is clear,
the dark hides things
everything's concealed.

What people are really afraid of,
what haunts their thoughts and dreams,
isn't the dark itself, but what we cannot see.

What lurks among the shadows
and creeps along the floor

what floats through the air above you
and hides behind the door.

The darkness itself isn't what scares me,
for that I certainly say

no, what scares me most
is what the darkness hides away.

I used to sit in bed at night
blankets wrapped up tight

hoping that the things that watched me
won't put up a fight.

Then I came to realize,

rather suddenly,

that if the darkness hid other things
it could certainly hide me.

Now I sleep at night,
completely at peace,
concealed by a fear I now release.

Memories

Easy to make,
Harder to find again

The Band room

The sound of instruments,
playing randomly and out of tune fills the halls

a hundred or so children,
blowing hot, fast air into metal and wooden tubes

but all it takes is a quick tap of the baton,
to bring order from the chaos.

Swish and flick,
a note is played

the cord resonates
bouncing off the walls of the small room.
It flies up into the rafters,
rings a few seconds,
then silence,
a perfect release.

The man standing before us smiles
it fills me with warmth
all that we want is to make him proud,
the words "well done" fall from his lips
and the whole room fills with smiling faces.

That's my favorite memory
of time well spent,
sitting in that band room
surrounded by friends,

playing, laughing, singing out of key
every day after school
my favorite place to be.

I look back on it now
thinking about the love, joy, sorrow we shared
remembering the words that stuck with me
words I didn't believe
now known to be true
"You will never find a home like this anywhere else,
not the same laughter,
the community,

the friends,
all fueled by the holy spirit
now till the end."
Music will forever be a part of me
as will the memories I made
the lessons I learned
and the people I touched.

I can't go back
and don't wish that I could
because that time
those endless hours of practice,
and love,
and joy,
brought me to where I am today
I wouldn't trade a single day of it for the world.

Ozark

Wake to the sound of silence,
the smell of fresh coffee,
the chill in the morning air.

Padded footsteps down the hall,
a plate pull quietly from the cabinet,
muffin in one hand
cup in the other,

the glass door slides open,
the smell from the lake wafts into the house,
the air is damp,
the birds sing.

The sun slowly rises above the hills
hitting the water
making it shimer.

The air warms,
as the coffee cools,

the house begins to stir,
the sound of voices,
but the spell of the morning lingers
as the dawn slowly fades.

Bailey

A yip and yap,
soft fur,
little nose,
tiny paws,
the puppy scurries across the floor.

All excitement,
no traction,
laughter, energy, joy,
the dog we would never get
made everyone happy.

Strokes

Blank, white, clean,
waiting, calling, whispering,
one stroke
two strokes
three
four,
the color spreads,
brilliant, vibrant, explosion.

They mix and they swirl
a symphony without sound
a picture forms, morphs, focus,
blur, blend, brush,
a landscape
a portrait
a fairytale
a dream
Painting creates new worlds
all you need is one, two, three.

Blue

That beautiful blue note sound
crisp, clean, clear
it resonates through the body
you feel it in your soul,

its deep and whole
and profound,
warm and rich
and round,

smooth as butter
cool like ice
soft as silk
tight like a vice

Jazz is a language
Blues is a tongue
the musician a mouthpiece
of that sweet soulful fun.

Lost

Warm vanilla,
dark chocolate,
morning coffee,
a dinner stew,
she was left with the memories of these things.
The cake was just a sponge
the drink was just wet
the soup had no flavor
the fruit had no flare
she was left wishing for something that was no longer there.
The sickness had taken it
her smell and her taste
she was left feeling that it all went to waste.

Found

A faded dusty box
in the back corner of a room
where the sun barely shines,

the attic is warm and inviting
unlike in the movies,
it has a peace within it
a clam place to reside.

And in that dusty box
are things some may hold dear,
other may want to keep them hidden
locked away in fear.

But you lift the lid
and open the box,
inside is something you lost

and what is this thing
but a memory,
it's faded and worn
a tad bit torn
but there all the same,

maybe it's happy
maybe it's sad
maybe it's nothing at all,
but a black and white image
of a time long past
one you had forgotten
one you found at last.

Death

Inevitable.

Freedom

A mother sat at the window overlooking the world.
Her hair was grey and thin,
her eyes tired and weak,
but her heart was content.

Then a child only ten came and sat by the mother.
"You're leaving." she said in a small tiny voice,
"Where will you go?"
Mother turned to her,
a smile in her eyes,

"I will go where you take me.
First, my body will return to the dust from whence it came.
Then you will take me to my homeland.
You must find the mountain that overlooks the beauty of God's earth
and releases my soul to it
so I may ride the wind and be free."

"But how will I find you?"

"If you listen hard enough
you will hear my voice in the breeze
and feel my guiding hand on your heart."

The child smiled as the door opened for the second time.
There stood a figure we all know well.
He held out his hand
and mother took it as she fell.
Then the child did as told
and took the mother to the highest peak,
and released her ashes so that she could be free.

The Truth of Life

One day, Life asked Death,
"Why do people love me but hate you?"
Death only smiled and said in reply,
"Let us ask this young man coming our way." As the man approached
Death called out to him and asked: "Which of us do you see as the most
beautiful?" The young man laughed and said, "well the lady of course. Life
is the most beautiful thing in the world." Death smiled again and sent him
on his way. As the years went by Life and Death watched the man grow and
face the challenges and hardships Life threw at him, as she does to us all.
And when he reached the age of ninety-eight Death sought him out and
said,
"Now may I ask who you see as the most beautiful?" The man looked up at
Death and smiled, "Death is the most beautiful gift that God gave to the
world." And Death greeted him with open arms. For the man had grown
old and weak but the years had given him wisdom. To him, the wonders
and beauty of Life had faded and he welcomed the lovely sight of Death at
his door. Death then turned to Life and said,
"To answer your question, people do not hate me and love you or find you
more beautiful than I. For love of Life is given at birth and love of Death is
found with age."

ABOUT THE AUTHOR

Anya has loved writing for as long as she can remember. As an artist, she likes to say that "writing is how we paint the world with words." In her free time, Anya is an avid reader, baker, Netflix binger, and lacrosse player. *A Study on Life* is her first published book, however, she has had previous works published by the American Library of Poetry. Anya would also like you to note that she despises talking about herself and will therefore keep this bio as short as possible while giving the reader a good look at her character.